Inner Awakening: The Journey of Spiritual Awareness

Preface

Welcome to "Inner Awakening: The Journey of Spiritual Awareness." In these pages, I invite you to embark on a journey beyond the boundaries of ordinary consciousness, towards the depths of the soul and the vastness of the inner universe.

This book is conceived with the intent to be a comprehensive and inspiring guide, offering you an itinerary that traverses various aspects of spiritual awareness. From explorations of the mind, body, and spirit to the profound connection with nature and the cosmos, to personal transcendence and a sense of oneness with the universe, each chapter is designed to nurture your spirit and guide you in discovering new perspectives.

The path undertaken is not merely a journey of knowledge but a dance with life itself. Through the pages of this book, I encourage you to immerse yourself in the awareness of the present moment, explore your inner self with curiosity, and connect with the beauty and wisdom of the surrounding nature.

Spiritual awareness is a personal and universal journey. Whether you are already immersed in a spiritual practice or beginning your journey, I hope these pages become a faithful companion in your inner exploration. May you find inspiration, solace, and illumination as you delve into the richness of your spiritual essence.

May this book become a guiding light in the darkness, leading you through challenges and illuminating the path towards a deeper awareness. Each page is an invitation to awaken your spirit and dance with the wonder of life.

Safe travels, explorer of the soul.
May inner awakening be the
melody accompanying every step
of your journey.

Chapter 1: Introduction

Author's Presentation

Welcome to this journey into spiritual awareness. I am delighted to accompany you on this profound and meaningful exploration of the spiritual dimension of our existence. My passion for spirituality arises from a personal journey of discovery, transformation, and connection with the deeper essence of life. Through the pages of this book, I will share with you not only my experience but also the knowledge and reflections gained along the way.

This is not just a book; it is an invitation to explore the depths of your soul and discover the potential for growth and fulfillment that resides within each of us. My hope is that this journey becomes a catalyst for significant personal transformation, leading you to embrace a deeper and more fulfilling spiritual awareness.

Preface on the Meaning of Spiritual Awareness

Modern life presents us with countless distractions and hectic commitments that often distance us from our true nature. Spiritual awareness is the key to reconnecting with that part of ourselves that goes beyond daily concerns and material challenges. In this chapter, we will explore together the profound meaning of spiritual awareness, beyond conventional definitions, unveiling a world of inner possibilities waiting to be discovered.

Spirituality is not confined to places of worship or ritual practices but is a personal journey toward understanding our purpose, connecting with the divine, and realizing our highest potential. Spiritual awareness provides the necessary

perspective to face challenges
with balance, appreciate the
beauty of human relationships,
and experience lasting inner
peace.

Objectives of the Book

This book has been written with
the intention of guiding you
through a journey of self-
exploration and spiritual growth.
The objectives are multifaceted
and include:

- **Illuminate the Meaning of
  Spiritual Awareness:** We
  will delve into a deeper
  understanding of what it
  truly means to be
  spiritually aware, going
  beyond superficial
  definitions and discovering
  the transformative
  potential of awareness.

- **Provide Practical Tools:** I
  will offer practical tools
  and exercises that you can

integrate into your daily life to cultivate a meaningful spiritual practice.

- **Explore Connection with the Universe:** We will investigate the link between spiritual awareness and connection with nature, the cosmos, and our surrounding environment.

- **Overcome Inner Challenges:** We will address emotional and psychological challenges that may hinder the spiritual journey, providing strategies to overcome and grow through them.

Through this book, I hope to inspire you to explore your spiritual potential, allowing you to live a more authentic, aware, and meaningful life. Prepare for a journey that will take you beyond the surfaces of daily life,

discovering your deeper essence
and the intrinsic beauty of the
spiritual journey. Safe travels!

Chapter 2: Definition of Spiritual Awareness

Exploring the Definition of Spiritual Awareness

At the heart of every spiritual quest lies spiritual awareness, a concept that goes beyond superficial definitions. Exploring spiritual awareness means delving into a deeper dimension of one's existence, embracing the mystery of being, and the connection with something greater than ourselves.

Spiritual awareness is the process of inner awakening, where we become aware of our most authentic essence and our connection to the universe. It is not a static dogma but rather a dynamic path of personal discovery, a journey that urges us to explore our inner selves with curiosity and openness. Through spiritual awareness, we gain a broader perspective on life, learning to live in the present with gratitude and compassion.

Differences between Spirituality and Religion

It is crucial to distinguish spiritual awareness from religion, as these two concepts, although overlapping, have distinct foundations and approaches. Spirituality is inherently personal and non-dogmatic, allowing for a variety of unique paths towards awareness. Religion, on the other hand, often incorporates an organized system of beliefs and shared ritual practices within a specific community.

Spiritual awareness does not require allegiance to a set of predetermined doctrines but encourages individual exploration of the divine and one's connection to it. In spirituality, the freedom to interpret and embrace transcendence personally is fundamental, allowing

practitioners to tailor their
practice to the unique needs of
their journey.

**The Importance of Awareness
in the Spiritual Journey**

Awareness is the fundamental
pillar upon which the spiritual
journey is built. It invites us to be
present in the current moment,
cultivate a deeper understanding
of ourselves, and explore our
connection to the divine. The
hectic pace of life and daily
challenges can easily distract us
from our true nature, but
awareness empowers us to return
to our center, to our most
authentic essence.

In the context of the spiritual
journey, awareness becomes a
tool of transformation. It enables
us to transcend the illusions of
the ego, embrace inner wisdom,
and navigate life's challenges with
grace. Through awareness, we
discover that the true meaning of

the spiritual journey is not only reaching a destination but embracing the journey itself with all its teachings and moments of growth.

In this chapter, we will explore the nuances of spiritual awareness, delving into its meaning and recognizing its importance in shaping our spiritual path. Get ready to discover a world of possibilities and open the doors to your ever-expanding spiritual awareness.

Chapter 3: Foundations of Spiritual Awareness

In our journey towards spiritual awareness, it is crucial to lay solid foundations upon which to build our practice. This chapter explores the key foundations that will guide us through the expansion of our spiritual awareness.

Key Concepts: Mindfulness, Presence, Acceptance

Mindfulness: The first fundamental pillar is mindfulness, the active and non-judgmental awareness of the present moment. Being mindful allows us to connect with the reality of our being, quieting the noise of past or future concerns. Through mindfulness, we learn to be fully present in every moment, recognizing the beauty and depth of life unfolding here and now.

Presence: Presence goes beyond simple awareness, urging us to fully immerse ourselves in the present moment with an open heart and a clear mind. Being present means wholeheartedly embracing what is happening without judgment, allowing a deeper connection with ourselves and the world around us.

Acceptance: Spiritual awareness embraces acceptance, an act of love towards oneself and others. Accepting reality without resistance frees us from the chains of attachment and allows us to flow with the natural course of life. Mindful acceptance is a crucial step on the spiritual path, enabling us to transform challenges into opportunities for growth.

Role of Meditation and Contemplation

Meditation and contemplation are powerful tools that guide us in discovering our inner foundations. Meditation, with its variety of approaches, provides a sanctuary to retreat from daily chaos and develop concentration, calmness, and mental clarity. Through meditation, we learn to observe our thoughts without identifying with them, creating space for awareness to flourish.

On the other hand, contemplation invites us to deeply reflect on significant themes, channeling our attention towards the exploration of inner answers. Through the regular practice of these disciplines, we develop the ability to look beyond superficial appearances and grasp the intrinsic truth of things.

Connecting Mind, Body, and Spirit

Our being is an intricate interweaving of mind, body, and spirit, and spiritual awareness aims to unite them in a harmonious symphony. The mind-body-spirit connection helps us understand that we are not separate entities but part of an interconnected whole. Practices such as yoga, mindful breathing, and sensory exploration guide us in this integration, opening doors to a deeper understanding of our being.

In this chapter, we will explore these foundations with the intention of providing you with the necessary tools to develop a conscious and sustainable practice. Be ready to immerse yourself in the depths of your awareness, as these foundations are the bedrock upon which you will build your spiritual journey.

Chapter 4: Exploring One's Inner Self

In the journey of spiritual awareness, the discovery of one's inner self is a crucial step. This chapter outlines the importance of exploring our inner world, providing tools and techniques to guide us through this adventure of self-discovery.

The Importance of Self-Reflection

Self-reflection is a powerful practice that allows us to delve deep within ourselves. It is an act of conscious awareness that enables us to explore our thoughts, emotions, and hidden motivations. Through self-reflection, we learn to discern between the voices of the mind and the authentic voice of our inner being.

This practice offers us the opportunity to better understand who we are beyond social masks and superficial identities. In self-reflection, we find the key to unlock the door to our inner self, paving the way for a deeper connection with our authentic selves.

Techniques to Explore One's Inner Self

- **Self-Observation Meditation:** Find a quiet place, sit comfortably, and close your eyes. Bring your attention to your breath and start observing your thoughts without judgment. Let the thoughts float like clouds in the sky of your mind, without clinging to any of them. This practice will help you develop a detached awareness of your thoughts.

- **Journal Writing:** Dedicate time each day to free writing in your journal. Explore your thoughts, emotions, and daily experiences. Journal writing is a mirror of your inner self, allowing you to clearly see thought patterns and reveal the deeper desires of your heart.

- **Sensory Awareness Practices:** Take a mindful walk, focusing your attention on what you perceive through your senses. Listen to sounds, observe the colors around you, feel the contact with nature. These sensory practices will help you tune into the present moment and deepen your connection with the surrounding environment.

Overcoming Emotional Blocks

During our inner exploration, we may encounter emotional blocks that hinder the flow of our awareness. Recognizing and overcoming these blocks is essential to release our inner energy and access deeper levels of self-understanding.

- **Forgiveness Practice:** Explore the power of forgiveness, both towards others and yourself. Forgiveness releases trapped emotional energy, paving the way for inner healing and spiritual rebirth.

- **Mindfulness of Emotions:** Practice mindfulness when experiencing intense emotions. Observe these emotions without identifying with them, allowing them to flow through you. This awareness will help you avoid emotional attachment and gain a deeper understanding of the transient nature of emotions.

Exploring one's inner self is an engaging and revealing journey. Through self-reflection and mindful practices, you can discover hidden layers of your being, opening the door to deeper awareness and a more authentic life. In the next chapter, we will continue this fascinating journey, exploring the connection with nature and the cosmos.

Chapter 5: Connection with Nature and the Cosmos

At the heart of spiritual awareness lies a profound connection with nature and the cosmos. This chapter explores the beauty and wisdom that emerge when we open our hearts and minds to the universe that surrounds us.

Spirituality as Connection with Nature

Nature is a tangible manifestation of the beauty and intrinsic harmony of the universe. Spirituality, seen as a connection with nature, invites us to rediscover our ancestral bond with the natural world. Through contemplation of the elements, the sounds of birds, the changing of seasons, and the sensation of the earth beneath our feet, we can reconnect with our spiritual roots.

Nature becomes a silent teacher, imparting the wisdom of patience, transformation, and the cyclical nature of life. Embracing this connection means acknowledging our impact on the environment and cultivating a respectful relationship with the Earth, making us conscious stewards of this wonder.

The Role of Cosmic Energies

Invisible yet potent cosmic energies permeate the universe and constantly surround us. These energies, often associated with concepts like prana, chi, or ki in various spiritual traditions, are considered sources of vitality and awareness. Exploring the role of these energies in the realm of spiritual awareness means opening up to the perception of a subtler and interconnected reality.

Consciously attuning to and directing these energies can become a source of balance and healing. Through meditation, mindful breathing, and conscious interaction with the environment, we can tune into cosmic energies, strengthening our connection with the vast fabric of the universe.

Practices to Strengthen the Bond with the World Around Us

- **Nature Meditation:** Find a quiet outdoor space, whether it's a park, forest, or meadow. Sit or lie down comfortably and immerse yourself in the beauty of the nature surrounding you. Nature meditation not only quiets the mind but also strengthens the spiritual bond with the natural world.

- **Nature Ceremonies:** Celebrate significant moments outdoors. Create personal rituals or participate in ceremonies that honor the beauty and power of nature. These ceremonies become bridges connecting your inner being with the essence of the Earth.

- **Grounding Practice:** Spend time walking barefoot on the earth or sitting in direct contact with the ground. This grounding act will connect you with earthly energies, promoting a sense of rootedness and stability.

Connection with nature and the cosmos is a fundamental piece in the mosaic of spiritual awareness. In this chapter, we have explored how this bond can enrich our spiritual lives, leading us to a deeper understanding of our role in the cosmic ecosystem. In the next chapter, we will tackle the challenge of overcoming inner

barriers and embracing
vulnerability on the spiritual
journey.

Chapter 6: Overcoming Inner Challenges

In the journey of spiritual awareness, we inevitably encounter inner challenges that test our inner strength and determination. This chapter explores the process of facing fears and uncertainties, discovering the transformative power of gratitude, and learning to turn challenges into precious opportunities for spiritual growth.

Facing Fears and Uncertainties

Fears and uncertainties are inevitable companions on our spiritual path. Confronting these challenges requires the courage to look within ourselves and explore the deep roots of our fears. It is an act of self-reflection that allows us to understand how fears can limit our spiritual growth.

Facing fears also means embracing uncertainty as an integral part of life. Spiritual awareness teaches us to cultivate trust in the process of life, even when we cannot see the path ahead. Accepting fears and embracing uncertainty become milestones in building our spiritual resilience.

The Power of Gratitude

Gratitude is a catalyzing force in transforming inner challenges. Through the practice of gratitude, we learn to shift our focus from lack to abundance. It is a potent antidote to discontent and fear, directing our attention to what is positive and meaningful in our lives.

Gratitude becomes a daily practice that connects us with the essence of life itself. When we recognize and appreciate blessings, even in small things, we open the door to joy and inner peace. In times of challenges, gratitude becomes a guiding light that helps us overcome inner darkness.

Transforming Challenges into Opportunities for Spiritual Growth

Every challenge, when approached with awareness, carries the opportunity for spiritual growth. Transforming challenges into opportunities requires a shift in perspective, a vision that looks beyond immediate pain and focuses on the lesson that can emerge from difficulty.

- **Mindfulness Practice in Difficult Moments:** When facing challenging times, practice non-judgmental mindfulness. Observe your reactions, emotions, and resistances. This act of self-reflection allows a deeper understanding of the inner dynamics that may contribute to the challenges we are experiencing.

- **Cultivating Resilience:** Resilience is the ability to adapt and grow despite adversity. Cultivating spiritual resilience means accepting that challenges are part of our journey and that we can overcome them with wisdom and inner strength.

- **Reflection on Transcendence:** In challenges, reflect on the possibility of transcending daily concerns. Look beyond the pain and find meaning in your experiences, connecting with the deeper dimension of your being.

Facing fears, cultivating gratitude, and transforming challenges into opportunities for spiritual growth are an ongoing process that accompanies us along our path. In the next chapter, we will explore the importance of relationships in our spiritual journey and how awareness can enrich human connections.

Chapter 7: Relationships and Spiritual Awareness

In the vast landscape of spiritual awareness, human relationships emerge as significant pillars intricately woven into the fabric of our journey. This chapter aims to explore the importance of relationships on the spiritual path, emphasizing conscious communication and compassion as keys to authentic connection and the shared experience of the spiritual journey with others.

The Importance of Relationships on the Spiritual Path

Human relationships serve as reflective mirrors of our consciousness and inner being. On our spiritual journey, they become fertile grounds for learning and growth. Connecting with others provides an opportunity to practice mindfulness in interpersonal situations, deepening our understanding of ourselves and others.

The act of loving, understanding, and supporting others becomes a spiritual practice in itself. Sharing experiences, peacefully resolving conflicts, and expressing gratitude within relationships contribute to creating a fertile ground for spiritual growth.

Conscious Communication and Compassion

Conscious communication is an essential component in building authentic and meaningful relationships. It involves listening attentively, responding empathetically, and speaking with clarity and sincerity. Mindful communication helps us overcome the barriers of misunderstanding and creates fertile ground for mutual respect.

Compassion, the beating heart of spiritual awareness, manifests in recognizing and alleviating the pain of others. It urges us to see beyond external differences and connect with humanity with an open heart. In relationships, compassion becomes a bridge that links our hearts, allowing us to share the joys and challenges of the spiritual journey together.

Sharing the Spiritual Journey with Others

Spirituality may often seem like a solitary path, but sharing the spiritual journey with others profoundly enriches the experience. Finding communities of kindred spirits, sharing spiritual ideas and practices, acts as a powerful catalyst for spiritual growth.

- **Spiritual Support Groups:** Participating in spiritual support groups provides a safe environment to

explore ideas, receive
support, and share the
challenges and victories of
the spiritual journey. These
groups become even more
crucial during difficult
times, offering a support
network where one feels
understood and accepted.

- **Intimate and Family
Relationships:** Close
relationships, such as
those with a partner,
family, or intimate friends,
become grounds for
significant spiritual growth.
Through conscious
communication and
sharing the inner journey, a
bond is created that goes
beyond the superficial,
contributing to personal
and collective growth.

- **The Act of Teaching and
Learning:** Teaching what
we have learned on our
spiritual journey and

learning from others enriches our understanding and provides new perspectives. This process of exchange contributes to building a community of shared learning and growth.

In the next chapter, we will explore daily spiritual practices that can be integrated into our everyday lives to cultivate continuous spiritual awareness. Awareness in relationships becomes a journey of mutual exchange, a precious gift that nourishes our spirit and enriches the fabric of our lives.

Chapter 8: Daily Spiritual Practices

In the whirlwind of our daily lives, spiritual awareness can serve as the compass guiding us toward deeper meaning and authentic connection. This chapter is dedicated to integrating spiritual awareness into everyday life, offering practical suggestions to maintain a regular practice and create meaningful personal rituals.

Integrating Spiritual Awareness into Daily Life

Spiritual awareness is not meant to reside solely in moments of meditation or contemplation but to permeate every aspect of our daily lives. Integrating it means bringing awareness into the present, both during daily activities and moments of reflection.

- **Breath Awareness:** Practicing breath awareness is a powerful way to anchor yourself in the present. Dedicate a few minutes each day to focus on your breath, feeling it flow in and out. This practice can be easily integrated into daily activities such as driving, walking, or cleaning.

- **Mindfulness in Meals:** Transform meals into opportunities for mindfulness. Take the time to appreciate the flavors, textures, and aromas of the food. Eat slowly, put away devices, and consciously connect with the nourishment entering your body.

- **Body Awareness:** Body awareness can be practiced at any time of the day. Pause periodically to notice sensations in your body. Be aware of posture, tensions, and physical sensations. This will help maintain a constant connection with your physical vehicle.

Practical Tips for Maintaining a Regular Practice

- **Morning Routine:** Create a morning routine that includes elements of spiritual awareness. It may involve breathing exercises, short meditation, or expressions of gratitude upon waking.

- **Periodic Reminders:** Set regular reminders on your phone or write reminder notes to prompt practicing awareness throughout the day. These reminders can serve as small rings connecting you to your spiritual commitment.

- **Short Practices Before Sleep:** Incorporate brief awareness practices before sleep, such as reflecting on the day, expressing gratitude for experiences, and breath awareness. This promotes a more restful sleep and a tranquil transition to the night.

Creating Meaningful Personal Rituals

Personal rituals provide structure for spiritual practice and instill a sense of sacredness in everyday life. Here are some ideas for creating meaningful personal rituals:

- **Morning Ritual:** Dedicate a brief ritual in the morning, perhaps lighting a candle, setting an intention for the day, and practicing a few minutes of meditation.

- **Gratitude Ritual:** Before bedtime, reflect on three things you are grateful for. You can write them in a journal or simply contemplate them silently.

- **Nature Ritual:** Connect with nature through a ritual, such as a mindful walk in the park or a moment of silence in the garden.

Integrating spiritual awareness into daily life requires commitment and consistent practice. Be open to experimenting and adapting these practices to your unique lifestyle. In the next chapter, we will explore the final stage of the spiritual journey: self-realization and the incorporation of awareness into the entirety of life.

Chapter 9: Transcendence and the Sense of Oneness

At the pinnacle of our spiritual journey, we enter the realm of personal transcendence, a place where the boundary between the individual self and the universe dissolves. This chapter explores the pursuit of personal transcendence, the profound desire for union with the universe, and the mystical experiences that can illuminate our path.

Exploring Personal Transcendence

Personal transcendence is the culmination of a spiritual journey, a step beyond the limited perception of the self. In this state of heightened awareness, a profound connection with the entirety of existence is experienced. Personal transcendence is not just a

moment but a continuous flow in which the self dissolves into the cosmic fabric, embracing unity with all that is.
This state of transcendence can be achieved through spiritual practices, profound meditation experiences, or moments of spontaneous enlightenment. Personal transcendence does not imply the denial of the individual self but rather its elevation to a broader level of awareness.

Seeking a Sense of Oneness with the Universe

The search for a sense of oneness with the universe is intrinsic to our human nature. Spiritual awareness urges us to overcome the illusions of separation and seek a deeper understanding of our connection to the entire cosmos. This quest is not only intellectual but also a matter of direct experience and awareness.

- **Union Practices:**
Practices such as
mindfulness meditation,
deep contemplation, and
exploration of energetic
connections can open the
door to the direct
perception of our
interconnectedness with
the universe.

- **Exploration of Collective
Consciousness:**
Reflecting on collective
consciousness and shared
experiences can reveal our
intrinsic part in the
evolution of human
consciousness. This helps
us understand that our
spiritual journey is a larger
piece of a universal
tapestry.

- **Non-Dualism Practice:**
Understanding non-
dualism, the perception
that the duality between
self and other is an illusion,

can guide us toward a deeper sense of oneness. This perspective invites us to transcend apparent divisions and recognize the fundamental unity of life.

Mystical Experiences and Spiritual Illuminations

Mystical experiences and spiritual illuminations are moments when transcendence becomes tangible. These moments can manifest in various forms, such as profound visions, transformative insights, or a profound sense of total unity with the universe. They are often described as extraordinary experiences of connection with the divine or ultimate reality.

- **Moments of Enlightenment:** Seeking moments of enlightenment may involve practicing deep meditations, intensive spiritual retreats, or prolonged periods of silence. These moments can lead to a clear understanding of the illusory nature of the ego and direct perception of ultimate reality.

- **Mystical Perceptions:** Mystical experiences may involve deep visions, states of ecstasy, or a profound sense of divine presence. These moments can radically transform the perception of self and the world, opening the door to a broader and more inclusive understanding of life.

- **Integration of Experiences:** After a mystical experience or a moment of enlightenment, the challenge is to integrate this awareness into everyday life. This may require a period of reflection and adjustment, bringing the awareness of transcendence into the details of daily life.

At the end of our journey, transcendence and the sense of oneness become the key to understanding the totality of life. In the final chapter, we will explore the meaning of self-realization and how spiritual awareness can be channeled to create a meaningful and fulfilling life.

Chapter 10: The Journey Continues

We conclude our spiritual journey with a reflection on the entire path, exploring the lessons learned, the meaning of continuous growth, and the invitation to pursue endless spiritual development.

Reflections on the Entire Journey

The spiritual journey has been a venture into the depths of the soul, an exploration of the boundaries of the self, and a continuous discovery of the meaning of life. In this concluding phase, we reflect on how each chapter has woven its thread into the fabric of our spiritual development.

- **Awareness and Interiority:** We began with awareness, exploring tools of self-reflection and inner awareness. This prepared us for the inner journey, opening the door to the discovery of the deeper self.

- **Connection with Nature and the Cosmos:** We delved into the connection with nature and cosmic energies, recognizing our part in the vast fabric of the universe. This led us to a broader understanding of our role in the cosmic ecosystem.

- **Overcoming Inner Challenges:** By facing fears, embracing gratitude, and transforming challenges into opportunities for growth, we strengthened our spiritual resilience. This

guided us through the
challenging phases of our
journey.

- **Relationships and
Spiritual Awareness:**
Human relationships
emerged as significant
sources of learning and
growth. Through mindful
communication,
compassion, and sharing
the spiritual journey with
others, we enriched our
connection with humanity.

- **Daily Spiritual Practices:**
We learned to integrate
spiritual awareness into
daily life, maintaining a
regular practice and
creating meaningful
personal rituals. This
guided us toward
continuous awareness in
the flow of everyday life.

- **Transcendence and the Sense of Oneness:** Lastly, we explored personal transcendence, the search for a sense of oneness with the universe, and mystical experiences. These culminating moments took us beyond the boundaries of the self, opening the door to a deeper understanding of life's fundamental unity.

Continuous Development and Adaptation

The spiritual journey does not conclude here; it is an eternal flow of growth and adaptation. Life itself is a continuous teacher, and every moment offers the opportunity to deepen our awareness and evolve as spiritual beings.

- **Learning from Daily Life:** Every experience, from daily challenges to fleeting

joys, can be a lesson.
Keeping our eyes open to
the wisdom of daily life
allows us to grow even in
seemingly insignificant
moments.

- **Adapting to Life Phases:**
The spiritual journey
adapts to different phases
of life. This may include
adjustments to family
responsibilities,
professional challenges, or
changes in health.
Flexibility in our spiritual
approach helps us
navigate the diverse
seasons of life.

- **Cultivating an Open
Heart:** The invitation is to
cultivate an open heart and
a curious mind. Spiritual
growth continues when we
are willing to learn from
others, explore new
perspectives, and let life

teach us its valuable
lessons.

Invitation to Continuous Spiritual Growth

The final invitation is to pursue continuous spiritual growth with humility and gratitude. Every step, every breath, is an opportunity to deepen our awareness and embrace the beauty of being alive. In the endless journey of spiritual growth, we discover that the journey itself is the treasure we seek.

In this concluding chapter, we acknowledge that the journey has no end; it is a continuous return to ourselves and the essence of the universe. May this journey be for you an endless source of inspiration, discovery, and transformation. Safe travels.

Epilogue: The Infinite Dance of Awareness

In the epilogue of this spiritual journey, let's pause to reflect on the infinite dance of awareness we have undertaken together. This chapter summarizes the key concepts we have explored and provides a warm encouragement to the reader in the continuous flow of their spiritual journey.

Summary of Key Concepts

- **Awareness and Interiority:** We began our journey by exploring awareness and interiority as the foundation of the spiritual path. The ability to look within and be present in the moment opened us to the discovery of our true selves.

- **Connection with Nature and the Cosmos:** Through

connection with nature and
cosmic energies, we
broadened our perception,
recognizing that we are an
integral part of the vast
fabric of the universe.
Spirituality as connection
enriched our bond with the
world around us.

- **Overcoming Inner
  Challenges:** We faced
  fears, embraced gratitude,
  and learned to transform
  challenges into
  opportunities for spiritual
  growth. Spiritual resilience
  became a valuable guide
  in overcoming inner
  darkness.

- **Relationships and
  Spiritual Awareness:**
  Human relationships
  emerged as fertile ground
  for spiritual growth.
  Mindful communication
  and sharing the spiritual
  journey with others

enriched our human
connection.

- **Daily Spiritual Practices:**
We learned to integrate
spiritual awareness into
daily life, creating regular
practices and meaningful
personal rituals. These
practices became bridges
between awareness and
the experience of everyday
life.

- **Transcendence and the
Sense of Oneness:** At the
culmination of our journey,
we explored personal
transcendence, the search
for a sense of oneness
with the universe, and
mystical experiences.
These moments of
elevation took us beyond
the boundary of the
individual self, opening the
door to a deeper
understanding of life.

Encouragement for the Reader on Their Spiritual Journey

As we approach the end of this book, the invitation is to keep the flame of awareness alive in your heart. The spiritual journey is not a destination but an eternal dance with life itself. Here are some words of encouragement for your path:

- **Embrace Change:** Life is a river of constant change. Embrace the flow of life with openness and trust, knowing that every moment offers the opportunity to learn and grow.

- **Cultivate Gratitude:** Gratitude is a magical key that opens the doors to joy and peace. Cultivate a grateful heart, recognizing blessings even in challenges, and you will discover infinite richness in your life.

- **Continuously Explore:** The spiritual journey is a continuous expansion of consciousness. Explore new perspectives, practices, and ideas. Be open to life's surprises and embrace the infinite wonder of the mystery that surrounds us.

- **Share Your Journey:** Your experiences are a precious gift to others. Share your spiritual journey with kindness and authenticity. In the process of sharing, you will discover deeper connections with those you encounter along the way.

- **Be Kind to Yourself:** The spiritual path can be challenging, but be kind to yourself. Accept

imperfections, celebrate
progress, and embrace
your uniqueness. You are
an evolving being.

The infinite dance of awareness
continues, and you are the
protagonist of this magnificent
choreography of life. May your
spiritual journey be enriched by
awareness, connection, and
continuous discovery. May each
step be a song, each breath a
prayer, and each moment a
celebration of the beauty of your
being. Thank you for being part of
this dance. Safe travels.

Appendix: Resources, Meditation, and Bibliography

In this appendix, you will find a valuable collection of resources for further exploration, a guide to meditation and recommended practices, along with a complete bibliography of sources cited throughout the book.

Useful Resources for Further Exploration

- **Recommended Books:**

- "The Power of Now" by Eckhart Tolle

- "Wherever You Go, There You Are" by Jon Kabat-Zinn

- "The Quantum Mind" by Amit Goswami

- **Websites and Online Communities:**

- Mindfulness.org

- Insight Timer - Meditation app with a wide range of guided meditations

- **Spiritual Podcasts:**

- "On Being with Krista Tippett"

- "The School of Greatness" with Lewis Howes

- **Documentaries and Films:**

- "Life Is Beautiful" - A film by Roberto Benigni celebrating the beauty of life even in the most challenging circumstances.

- "Samsara" - A wordless documentary exploring the

connection between humans and the planet.

Guide to Meditation and Recommended Practices

- **Breath Meditation:**

- Find a quiet place, sit comfortably, and focus your attention on your breath. Observe the inhalation and exhalation mindfully.

- **Gratitude Meditation:**

- Before bedtime, reflect on three things you are grateful for. Focus on these gratitudes as you drift into sleep.

- **Mindful Walking:**

- Try walking mindfully, paying attention to the movement of your feet, the contact with the ground, and the sensation of your body in motion.

- **Open-Heart Meditation:**

- Sit in a comfortable position, place one hand on your heart, and breathe mindfully. Imagine a flow of love entering and leaving your heart.

Bibliography and Citations

- Tolle, Eckhart. "The Power of Now." New World Library, 1997.

- Kabat-Zinn, Jon. "Wherever You Go, There You Are." Hyperion, 1994.

- Goswami, Amit. "The Quantum Mind." Hampton Roads Publishing, 2007.

Quotes throughout the book are drawn from the works of various authors and spiritual teachers, including but not limited to Eckhart Tolle, Jon Kabat-Zinn, and Amit Goswami. Specific sources are indicated in the context of the quotes.

The appendix is intended as a practical guide and resource for those wishing to further explore the topics covered in the book. The suggested resources, meditation practices, and bibliography are a starting point for a personal journey of exploration and spiritual growth. Happy exploration!